FamilyFun Birthday Cakes

EDITED BY

DEANNA F. COOK

AND THE EXPERTS AT

FamilyFun MAGAZINE

EDITIONS

NEW YORK

FamilyFun
Birthday
Cakes

**FAMILYFUN
BOOK EDITORS**
Deanna F. Cook
Barbara Findlen
Grace Ganssle
Alexandra Kennedy

COPY EDITOR
Faye Wolfe

EDITORIAL ASSISTANTS
Jean Graham
Heather Johnson

ART DIRECTOR
Mark Mantegna

**CONTRIBUTING
EDITORS**
Jonathan Adolph
Nicole Blasenak
Dawn Chipman
Ann Hallock
Gregory Lauzon
Cindy A. Littlefield

**PRODUCTION
EDITORS**
Jennifer Mayer
Dana Stiepock

**TECHNOLOGY
COORDINATOR**
Tom Lepper

**IMPRESS, INC.
CREATIVE DIRECTOR**
Hans Teensma

DESIGN DIRECTOR
Carolyn Eckert

PROJECTS DIRECTOR
Lisa Newman

ART ASSOCIATE
Jen Darcy

This book is dedicated to *FamilyFun*'s avid bakers everywhere.

All of the cakes in this book were previously published in *FamilyFun* magazine. *FamilyFun* is a division of Disney Publishing Worldwide. To order a subscription, call 800-289-4849.

The staffs of *FamilyFun* and Impress, Inc. conceived and produced *FamilyFun Birthday Cakes* at 244 Main Street, Northampton, Massachusetts 01060, in collaboration with Disney Editions, 114 Fifth Avenue, New York, New York 10011-5690.

ISBN 0-7868-5398-0

First Edition
10 9 8 7 6 5 4 3 2
Library of Congress Cataloging-in-Publication Data on file.

Special thanks to the following *FamilyFun* magazine writers for their wonderful recipes: Cynthia Caldwell, Sharon Cindrich, Tobye Cook, Julia Lynch, Joyce Rita Malley, Rebecca Lazear Okrent, and Emily B. Todd.

We also extend our gratitude to *FamilyFun*'s many creative readers who shared with us their ideas for baking birthday cakes with their families: Debbie Abbott, Kim Arant, Sidra Baranoski, Shelley Collette, Lonnie Davis, Michelle Fehlman, Gail Fournier, Wendy Griffith, Randy Harris, Caroline Huntress, Martha Kimmel, Karin Overby, Sandy Parrott, Patty Reasinger, Julie Reimer, Meg Ryan, Andrea Schaper, Carrie Sharp, Kirsten Son, Melissa Specht, Jennifer Stansbury, Teresa and Nathan Strong, M. Lynne Taylor, Cynthia Telsey, Karen and Gregory Terry, Tracy Tucker, Darla Volbrecht, Nancy Wallace, and Norma Parker Wilson.

This book would not have been possible without the talented *FamilyFun* magazine staff, who edited and art-directed all of the original work. In addition to the book staff at left, we'd like to acknowledge the following staff members: Douglas Bantz, Jodi Butler, Terry Carr, Moira Greto, Michael Grinley, Ginger Barr Heafey, Heather Humble, Melanie Jolicoeur, Elaine Kehoe, Laura MacKay, Adrienne Stolarz, Mike Trotman, Ellen Harter Wall, Katherine Whittemore, and Sandra L. Wickland. We also would like to thank our partners at Disney Editions, especially Wendy Lefkon, Jody Revenson, and Marybeth Tregarthen.

About our major contributors:
Deanna F. Cook, Creative Development Director of *FamilyFun,* is the editor of the *FamilyFun* book series, which includes the *FamilyFun Cookbook* and *FamilyFun Parties,* from Disney Editions. She has baked many cakes in her Florence, Massachusetts, kitchen for her daughters, Ella and Maisie.

Cynthia Caldwell is a food stylist and writer who developed many of the cakes in this book. An avid baker since getting an Easy-Bake Oven when she was six, Cynthia now uses a real oven to create cakes for her husband, Shawn, and their children, Isabelle and Russell, in Whately, Massachusetts.

Table of Contents

PJ Kids Cupcakes,
page 43

Introduction

WHAT MAKES A birthday cake so magical? Is it the flickering candles in a darkened room? The "Happy Birthday" song? The birthday wish? Yes, all that — and the fact that a personalized birthday cake makes every kid feel incredibly special. So it's only natural that we parents go out of our way to bake birthday cakes for our kids every year.

At *FamilyFun* magazine, baking creative birthday cakes is an annual tradition. Each year, we feature a special birthday issue with cakes that are almost too clever to eat. Our readers and staff members have cooked up cupcake tea sets, chocolate pirate ships, and even edible swimming pools. And now we've collected the best of the bunch in this book.

Princess Cake,
page 15

10 Reasons to Bake a CAKE

Need a reason to bake, rather than buy, a birthday cake? Read our top-ten list below. We think you'll be sweetly persuaded to cook up something that money just can't buy.

1. **It's not hard.** You don't need to be an expert chef to bake one of our birthday cakes. A few basic pans and our fool-proof cake recipes are all you need.

2. **It makes your whole house smell good.** Remember how sweet and buttery your grandmother's house smelled when she baked you a cake?

3. **It can be custom-made.** Sure, the square cake with the cursive lettering looks nice, but a homemade cake can be tailored to the party theme — a ballerina for a dance party, a dump truck for a construction party . . . you get the picture.

4. **It tastes better than store-bought.** Unlike its synthetic, spongy cousin, the home-baked cake tastes good to the last bite.

4

Slippery Snake,
Page 56

Our designs may look like works of art, but they won't keep you in the kitchen all day. They require only a few clever cuts in a freshly baked cake, plus some artful frosting and colorful candies. You don't even need to buy any specialty pans. Most important, these sweet treats allow plenty of room for you to add your own creative touches.

With the help of this birthday cake handbook, the rest of your birthday planning, we hope, will be a piece of cake.

— The editors of *FamilyFun*

5. **You get to take the first bite.** When the cake is still warm, you can cut a strip from the side and eat it, and no one will ever notice.

6. **You'll look like the world's most creative parent.** Just follow our simple designs, and you'll be transformed from family cook to master pastry chef.

7. **It's good, old-fashioned fun.** Pull out the apron, crank the tunes, and stay home instead of hitting the bakery.

8. **It's fun for the kids.** Invite the birthday child's older sibling to be your sous-chef, or make cake-decorating a party activity.

9. **It'll be a golden photo opportunity.** A shot of the birthday child, in all her glory, blowing out the candles makes a splash in the family album.

10. **It'll be the hit of your child's birthday.**

Bake Me a Cake

ALL OF THE designs in this book begin with a basic cake — made either from a store-bought mix or from scratch. Here, we offer recipes for our favorite yellow, chocolate, banana, and carrot cakes. The batter can be baked in all sorts of ovenproof pans or bowls. For specific times, see the recipes.

Yellow Birthday Cake

This classic yellow cake is rich and buttery without being too sweet. It's sturdy enough to be cut into our cake shapes — and it won't fall apart when you frost it.

- $^3/_4$ cup butter, at room temperature
- 2 cups sugar
- 4 large eggs, separated
- 2 teaspoons vanilla extract
- $2^3/_4$ cups all-purpose flour
- $1^1/_2$ teaspoons baking powder
- $^1/_2$ teaspoon baking soda
- $^1/_4$ teaspoon salt
- 1 cup buttermilk

Preheat the oven to 350°. Butter and lightly flour the cake pans (see the following list of pan sizes).

Cream the butter for 1 to 2 minutes; add the sugar and cream for another 2 minutes. Add the egg yolks and beat for another minute or until the mixture appears light and fluffy.

Beat in the vanilla extract.

In a separate bowl, mix the flour, baking powder, baking soda, and salt. Add about a third of the flour mixture to the butter-sugar mixture and mix well. Then, mixing (but not overbeating) after each addition, add half of the buttermilk, followed by another third of the flour, then the remaining buttermilk, and finally the last of the flour.

Beat the egg whites until stiff. Gently fold them into the batter with a rubber spatula. Pour the batter into the prepared pans. Bake according to the times listed below, or until a toothpick inserted in the center comes out clean. Serves 8 to 10.

* Two 8- or 9-inch rounds or squares; bake for 45 minutes
* One 13- by 9- by 2-inch pan; bake for 45 minutes
* Two 12-cup cupcake tins; bake for 20 minutes
* Two dome cakes, baked in 1¹/₂-quart ovenproof bowls (stainless steel or Pyrex) for 55 minutes
* Two 8¹/₂- by 4¹/₂-inch loaf pans; bake for 45 minutes

Chocolate Cake

This devil's food recipe makes a moist cake, perfect for a chocolate lover's birthday party.

1¹/₂ cups water
4 ounces unsweetened chocolate
¹/₃ cup cocoa powder
1 cup canola oil
1 cup granulated sugar
³/₄ cup packed brown sugar
3 large eggs
1 teaspoon vanilla extract
2¹/₂ cups all-purpose flour
1¹/₂ teaspoons baking soda
1 teaspoon baking powder
¹/₄ teaspoon salt

Preheat the oven to 350°. Butter and lightly flour the cake pans (see the following list of pan sizes).

In a microwave-safe liquid measuring cup, measure 1½ cups water. Add the unsweetened chocolate to the water. Microwave for 2 to 3 minutes, stirring after 1½ minutes, or until the chocolate has melted. Transfer to a medium-size bowl and whisk until smooth. Whisk in the cocoa and set the mixture aside.

In a large mixing bowl, beat the oil, sugars, eggs, and vanilla extract together on high for 2 to 3 minutes, or until light and fluffy.

In a separate bowl, stir together the flour, baking soda, baking powder, and salt. Add the flour mixture and chocolate mixture alternately to the oil mixture, stirring well after each addition. When all the ingredi-

Tips for Better Cake-baking

* Always preheat your oven at least 12 to 15 minutes before baking the cake.
* Use the best ingredients available: high-quality butter, fresh eggs, and new baking powder.
* Measure ingredients (especially baking powder and baking soda!) precisely.
* Be sure to cream the butter and sugar well — this step is what gives a cake its light and smooth texture.
* To ensure an easy release from the cake pan, butter the bottom and sides, add a little flour, and shake it around, lightly knocking out any excess. Or, use a cooking spray, such as Pam or Baker's Joy.
* For extra-smooth cake bottoms (and guaranteed release), cut a piece of parchment or waxed paper to fit the pan. Grease the paper and the pan sides, then lightly flour.
* Most cakes should be baked on the middle rack of the oven. Do not crowd the cake pans — the cakes won't cook evenly.
* Test for doneness: Bake the cake until a toothpick inserted in the center comes out clean.

7

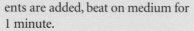

Birthday Tradition

"For each of our three children, Tom, 11, Ruth, 9, and Sam, 5, we have a photo album of their birthday cakes. We all enjoy looking at the pictures (remember the year Sam wanted a dog and got a dog cake?). The albums have turned into a record not just of the cakes, but of our children's changing interests as they grow."

— Meg Ryan
FamilyFun reader

ents are added, beat on medium for 1 minute.

Pour the cake batter into the prepared pans. Bake according to the times listed below, or until a toothpick inserted in the middle comes out clean. Serves 8 to 10.

* Two 8- or 9-inch rounds or squares; bake for 35 minutes
* One 13- by 9- by 2-inch pan; bake for 40 minutes
* Two 12-cup cupcake tins; bake for 20 minutes
* Two dome cakes, baked in 1½-quart bowls for 55 minutes
* One dome cake, baked in a 2½-quart bowl for 1 hour 20 minutes
* Two 8½- by 4½-inch loaf pans; bake for 45 minutes

Best Banana Cake

This banana cake will drive your party guests wild with its moist, delicious, banana-y taste. It is not too sweet, making it the perfect cake for a first birthday.

½ cup butter
1 cup sugar
2 eggs
2 cups all-purpose flour
1 teaspoon cream of tartar
1 teaspoon baking soda
¼ teaspoon salt
½ cup sour cream
3 ripe bananas, mashed (about 1 cup)
1 teaspoon vanilla extract
½ cup toasted wheat germ
⅔ cup chopped pecans (optional)

Preheat the oven to 350°. Butter and lightly flour the cake pans (see the following list of pan sizes). Cream the butter and sugar until light and fluffy. Add the eggs one at a time, beating well after each addition.

Sift together the dry ingredients. Mix the sour cream, bananas, and vanilla extract. Alternately add the dry ingredients and the sour-cream mixture to the butter mixture. Fold in the wheat germ and, if desired, the pecans.

Pour the batter into the prepared pans and bake according to the times below, or until a toothpick inserted in the center comes out clean. Serves 8 to 10.

* Two 8- or 9-inch rounds or squares; bake for 35 minutes
* One 13- by 9- by 2-inch pan; bake for 35 minutes
* Two 12-cup cupcake tins; bake for 20 minutes
* Two dome cakes, baked in 1½-quart bowls for 45 to 48 minutes
* One dome cake, baked in a 2½-quart

bowl for 1 hour and 15 minutes
* Two 8¹/₂- by 4¹/₂-inch loaf pans for 45 minutes

Carrot Cake

This cake is so delicious, your birthday child will never know it's healthier (at least a little) than your standard white cake.

- 2   cups grated carrot
    Juice of 1 lemon
- ¹/₂ teaspoon lemon zest
- ¹/₂ cup raisins
- ¹/₂ cup chopped walnuts, optional
- 2   cups packed light brown sugar
- 3   eggs, lightly beaten
- 1   teaspoon vanilla extract
- ¹/₂ cup buttermilk
- ¹/₂ cup vegetable oil
- ¹/₄ cup honey
- 2   cups all-purpose flour (or 1 cup each of white and whole wheat)
- 1   teaspoon cinnamon
- 1   teaspoon baking soda
- ¹/₂ teaspoon salt
- ¹/₂ teaspoon baking powder

Preheat the oven to 350°. Butter and lightly flour the cake pans (see the following list of pan sizes). Sprinkle the carrots with the lemon juice and stir in the zest; add the raisins and, if desired, walnuts, and set aside.

In an electric mixer or food processor, cream the brown sugar, eggs, vanilla extract, buttermilk, oil, and honey. Sift together the dry ingredients and gradually add them to the mixture, stirring just until smooth. Stir the carrot mixture evenly into the batter and pour into prepared pans.

Bake according to the times listed below, or until the top feels firm to the touch. Wait for the cakes to cool before removing them from the pans. Serves 8 to 10.

* Two 8- or 9-inch rounds or squares; bake for 35 minutes
* One 13- by 9- by 2-inch pan; bake for 40 minutes
* Two 12-cup cupcake tins; bake for 20 minutes
* Two dome cakes, baked in 1¹/₂-quart bowls for 55 minutes
* One dome cake, baked in a 2¹/₂-quart bowl for 1 hour and 15 minutes
* Two 8¹/₂- by 4¹/₂-inch loaf pans for 45 minutes

Tips for Cutting Cakes

* If you plan to cut your cake into a shape, it is helpful to bake your cake a day in advance. (Fresh cakes can be too soft to work with.)
* Start with a cold cake (refrigerate or partially freeze the baked cake before cutting it into a shape).
* Use a serrated knife in a gentle sawing motion.
* If your cake has a rounded top, you can cut it off with a serrated knife. Flip the cake so the cut side is the bottom and the smooth bottom is now the top.
* Before frosting your cakes, turn them out onto a large platter or cutting board. You can also purchase inexpensive cardboard cake rounds and rectangles at party-supply stores. (They come in a variety of sizes.)

Frosting Made Easy

The Icing on the Cake

* To keep your base clean while you frost your cake, tuck strips of waxed paper under the cake edges. When you're finished frosting, carefully slip them out.
* To prevent the cake from slipping while you frost it, dab a little frosting onto the platter before you place the cake down.
* For a crumb-free frosting, take a tip from the pros and crumb-coat your cake. To do this, spread a very thin layer of frosting on the cake, then refrigerate it. When the frosting is hard, frost and decorate the cake.
* For a smooth-frosted cake, use a straight-edged metal spatula. Frost the top of the cake first, beginning with a pile of frosting in the center and spreading it out to the sides. Next, frost the sides of the cake, working from top to bottom.
* To smooth frosting, run the spatula at a slight angle across the top of the cake (you can dip it in a glass of hot water first). Wipe off any excess frosting, then repeat on the sides. The trick is to use a single motion across the cake, rather than several small ones.

Buttercream Frosting

Although any of our cakes can be made with store-bought frosting, this homemade version, quick and easy to prepare, tastes better. Plus, it can be flavored in any way the birthday child fancies.

> 1 cup unsalted butter, at
>   room temperature
> 3½ cups sifted confectioners' sugar
> 1 teaspoon vanilla extract
> 2 to 4 tablespoons milk

With an electric mixer, beat the butter, confectioners' sugar, and vanilla extract at low speed. Add in the milk bit by bit until the mixture has reached a spreadable consistency. Makes about 3 cups.

Chocolate Frosting: Substitute 1 cup of cocoa powder for an equal amount of confectioners' sugar.

Lemon Frosting: Substitute 1 teaspoon lemon extract for the vanilla extract and add the finely grated zest of 1 lemon. Substitute ½ to 1 tablespoon of the milk with lemon juice.

Cream Cheese Frosting: Substitute 4 to 6 ounces of cream cheese for ½ cup of butter. Beat in an additional ½ to 1 cup confectioners' sugar.

Strawberry or Raspberry Frosting: Add ¼ cup of seedless strawberry or raspberry jam to the basic frosting recipe.

Colored Frosting

For a personal touch, tint your frosting the birthday child's favorite colors. For vibrant-colored frosting, use paste food colors, which are available at party-supply stores. Add dabs of the paste to your frosting with a toothpick — and keep in mind that a little paste gives a lot of color.

Decorators' Icing & Gel Icing

To write messages or draw pictures on a cake, use store-bought tubes of icing. Gel icing is shiny and smooth; decorators' icing resembles colored frosting. You can also color and pipe on our Buttercream Frosting. To do this, place the frosting in a Ziplock bag, cut off a tiny end of one corner, and squeeze out the frosting. If you decorate cakes often, you might want to invest in a cake-decorating kit and disposable pastry bags (see right).

Finishing Touches

Candy Decorations

For many of our cakes, we used bright, colorful candy decorations. You don't need to buy a lot of candy — pick up small bags at the checkout counter of your grocery store or purchase candy by the pound. Let the shapes and colors of the candies inspire you. LifeSavers become inner tubes for a pool party; fruit leather looks like a dog's tongue or collar; cotton candy is perfect for a ballerina's tutu.

Cookies & Crackers

Hit the cookie and cracker aisle of your local grocery store and look for graham crackers for the sleeping bags on page 54 or cookies for the train wheels on page 28. Crush cookie crumbs for the dirt on the Bug Mountain Cake on page 32.

Toys & Favors

Several of our cakes are decorated with children's toys, such as toy pirates on the pirate ship on page 24 or cars in the racetrack on page 49. Smaller toys placed on top of cupcakes also make terrific party favors. (Note: Be sure your toys are washed.)

Cake Novelties

Check your local party store or visit one online (see page 63) to find hundreds of inexpensive cake novelties, such as the cake doll on page 15 or the plastic swimmers on page 19.

Edible Decorations

At party-supply stores, you will also find numerous edible decorations. Look for sprinkles and sugars in every color of the rainbow, tiny edible flowers, edible glitter, and even candy eyes made of sugar.

Cake Decorating 101

With a pastry bag, a few decorating tips, and frosting, you can create all kinds of playful or intricate designs. Here are some suggestions for using the Wilton cake-decorating tips, available at party-supply stores and www.wilton.com (see page 63).

Round Tip #3: Works well for writing messages, drawing or outlining shapes, and making dots.

Star Tip #16: For mini flowers, simply hold the bag upright, press out a dab of frosting onto the cake, then lift the tip away. The star tip is also great for zigzag borders.

Star Tip #21: Ideal for shaping shells or scalloped borders. Hold the bag at a 45-degree angle, squeeze out frosting until it fans out, then slowly decrease the pressure and raise the bag from the cake.

Leaf Tip #67: Creates basic or ruffled leaves. Hold the bag at a 45-degree angle so that the tip opening is horizontal, squeeze out frosting, and slowly pull up the tip when you have the desired leaf length.

Snorkeler Cake

We think this cherubic-faced snorkeler will turn heads at any pool party (and the cake's decorations — a new mask and snorkel — make a terrific birthday present). We couldn't resist the original design, fashioned by *FamilyFun* reader Cynthia Telsey of Englewood, Colorado, for her son Matthew's eighth birthday party. We made our diver with chocolate frosting and Hershey's Kisses, but you could use a variety of frostings and candy options to make the cake look like your child.

WHAT YOU NEED
- 2 baked 9-inch round cakes
- 2 to 3 cups chocolate frosting
  Hershey's Kisses
- 2 green LifeSavers Gummies
- 2 blue M&M's
- 1 piece red shoestring licorice
- 1 orange gumdrop
  New snorkel and diving mask, washed with soap and water

WHAT YOU DO
Layer and frost the cakes. Unwrap the Kisses and place them around the top for hair. Add the LifeSavers Gummies and M&M's for the eyes, the licorice for the mouth, and the gumdrop for a nose. Remove or unfasten the strap on the diving mask, then place it over the face and lay the snorkel next to cake. Serves 8 to 10.

Under the Sea Cake

In Chippewa Falls, Wisconsin, both Brianna Volbrecht and her sister, Kersten, have fish tanks in their rooms, so mom Darla knew an aquarium cake would be a natural choice for Brianna's sixth birthday party. This whimsical underwater scene can be decorated in the swish of a mermaid's tail with just one color frosting and a handful of candy. **Tip:** If you have trouble finding candy rocks or seashells, see page 63.

WHAT YOU NEED

1. baked 13- by 9- by 2-inch cake
2. to 3 cups blue frosting
   Green apple Sour Belts
   Blue and/or green fruit leather
   Candy rocks
   Candy seashells
   Mini Swedish fish
   Sour tropical fish
   Gummy sea creatures, such as
     fish, sharks, and octopuses

WHAT YOU DO

Spread the blue frosting on the cake. To create plants, roll or twist various lengths of Sour Belts and fruit leather before placing them on the cake. Place candy rocks and seashells along the bottom. Finish off your underwater scene by arranging schools of gummy fish, sharks, and other deep-sea dwellers. Serves 8 to 10.

Party Plan

"My son's aquarium party was the best ever. The kids each brought a fish to stock his new tank. Then they stenciled fish T-shirts, made paper fish, and ate an aquarium cake."

—Patty Reasinger,
FamilyFun reader

Castle Cake

WE'RE QUITE SURE every princess we know will want this glittery castle cake for her birthday. *FamilyFun* reader Sidra Baranoski of South Deerfield, Massachusetts, created this castle for her niece Alexxis's fairy-tale birthday party. **Tip:** Although this cake could surely feed an entire royal court, you can make a smaller version by eliminating a layer or two.

WHAT YOU NEED

- 5 baked 8-inch square cakes
- 5 to 7 cups white frosting
- 5 sugar cones
- Purple and pink edible glitter or sugar crystals
- 1/2 cup pink frosting
- Yellow mini jawbreakers
- White and purple gumdrops
- Pink Good & Plenty
- Pink or red gel icing
- Mini candy hearts
- Red sprinkles
- Colored paper and tape
- 5 toothpicks

WHAT YOU DO

Cut one cake into 4 equal pieces and arrange 3 of them on top of the 4 other whole cakes, as shown, securing with frosting. (**Tip:** Cut up the extra cake piece for nibblers.) Spread the castle and cones with the white frosting, then sprinkle the cones with edible glitter and set them on the castle. With a pastry bag fitted with a writing tip, create pink frosting corner pillars and a door accented with mini jawbreakers. Set the gumdrops and Good & Plenty around the castle ledge, then add decorative loops of gel icing topped with the mini candy hearts. Finally, add the sprinkles around the top of the castle and top the cone turrets with flags cut from the colored paper and taped to the toothpicks. Serves 20 to 24.

Princess Cake

SERVE THIS FAIRY-TALE cake at a birthday celebration, and your child and her guests are sure to have a ball. You can find cake dolls at most party or cake decorating stores (or see page 63) for about $3.

WHAT YOU NEED
- 2 baked 9-inch round cakes
- 1 baked dome cake (baked in a 2¹/₂-quart bowl)
- 4 cups white frosting
  Red food coloring
  Gel icing
  Cake doll

WHAT YOU DO
Stack and lightly frost the two round cakes and then the dome cake (flat side down) on a serving plate to form a skirt. After the frosting firms up (you may have to chill the cake for a while), tint the remaining frosting with food coloring and spread it on the upper two thirds of the skirt. Pipe on decorative gel icing trim. Then press the waist of the cake doll into the center of the cake. Dress her in a frosting bodice, and she's ready to make her debut at the party. Serves 16 to 18.

Froggy Cupcake

Little party-goers will leap over each other to get to these edible bullfrogs.

WHAT YOU NEED
- 1 baked cupcake
  Blue frosting
- 1 large green gumdrop
- 2 white chocolate chips
  Black decorators' icing

First, cover the cupcake with the blue frosting. Slice the large green gumdrop in half. Press the tip of a white chocolate chip into the cut surface of each half, centering it near the bottom edge. Squirt a dab of black decorators' icing onto each chip. Then press the frog eyes into the frosting.

15

Barnyard Buddies

FAMILY FUN READER Michelle Fehlman needed a dessert for her son Andrew's first birthday party that was both playful and big enough to feed her large Phelan, California, family. She found this adorable menagerie of cakes to be the perfect solution.

WHAT YOU NEED

- 3 baked dome cakes (baked in 1-quart bowls)
- 3 baked 9-inch round cakes
- 10 baked cupcakes

Pig decorations

- 2 to 3 cups pink frosting
- 2 green Hi-C Fruit Slices
- 1 pink Hi-C Fruit Slice
- 2 Jujubes
- 2 Jujyfruits
  Red shoestring licorice
- 1 red Sour Belt

Cow decorations

- 2 to 3 cups white frosting
- 1 cup chocolate frosting
- 2 malted milk balls
- 2 black gumdrops
- ½ red Hi-C Fruit Slice
- 1 pink Hi-C Fruit Slice, cut into 4 pieces
  Black shoestring licorice

Sheep decorations

- 2 to 3 cups white frosting
- 3½ cups mini marshmallows
- 1 cup chocolate frosting
- 2 Jujyfruits
- 1 nonpareil
  Red shoestring licorice

WHAT YOU DO

For the basic shape, set a dome cake flat side down in the center of a round cake and secure with frosting, as shown. Cut 1 cupcake in half and place it as shown for the ears, then arrange 2 more cupcakes as legs. For the pig, add a cupcake snout. Each cake serves 10.

Pig: Frost the cakes and cupcakes pink. Decorate as shown, using the green fruit slices for hooves, the pink fruit slice for the mouth, the Jujubes for the nose, the Jujyfruits for the eyes, and the licorice for the ears and eyelashes. Finish off your little piggie with a curly Sour Belt tail.

Cow: Frost the cakes and cupcakes white, adding random chocolate frosting "spots." Decorate as shown, using the malted milk balls for eyes, the gumdrops for the nose, the red Fruit Slice piece for the mouth, pink Fruit Slice pieces for the ears, and the licorice for the hooves and eyelashes.

Sheep: Frost the cakes (except for a triangular face area), the outsides of the ears, and the top halves of the hooves with the white frosting, then cover with mini marshmallows. Use a pastry bag (or a plastic bag with one corner cut off) to pipe small dollops of chocolate frosting onto the face, the bottom halves of the hooves, and the centers of the ears. Decorate as shown, using the Jujyfruits for eyes, the nonpareil for a nose, and the licorice for the mouth.

NATURE

Hawaiian Beach Cake

WANT TO MAKE a big splash at your child's Hawaiian luau? Serve this beachy cake, complete with blue frosting waves, graham cracker sand, and hula dancers shimmying around a birthday candle bonfire. To find the plastic novelties and other beach treasures, visit your local party store or see page 63.

WHAT YOU NEED

1	baked 13- by 9- by 2-inch cake
2½	cups blue frosting
¼	cup white frosting
1	cup graham cracker crumbs
	Candy rocks
	Birthday candles
	Plastic Hawaiian dancers
	Candy flower sprinkles
	Plastic palm trees
	Fruit Stripe gum
	Plastic swimmers
	LifeSavers
	Sour tape, cut into 1-inch lengths
	Paper umbrella
	Plastic dolphin or gummy fish

WHAT YOU DO

Coat the entire cake with a thin layer of blue frosting. Swirl extra blue frosting on two thirds of the cake to create the ocean with waves and a curvy shoreline. Add whitecaps by squirting white frosting through a pastry bag.

To make the sandy beach, sprinkle graham cracker crumbs on the remaining third of the cake (the crumbs will stick to the thin layer of frosting).

Next, let your kids help you turn the cake into a bustling beach. Arrange a circle of candy rocks around a candle bonfire. Add Hawaiian dancers, a candy flower path, plastic palm trees, Fruit Stripe gum surfboards, plastic swimmers, LifeSavers inner tubes, sour tape beach blankets, and a paper umbrella. Don't forget to stock the ocean with edible and decorative sea creatures. Serves 8 to 10.

Beach Bash Cupcake

Even if you don't live near the waterfront, we're "shore" your family will enjoy this sweet taste of the sea.

WHAT YOU NEED

1	baked cupcake
	Blue frosting
	White frosting
	Graham cracker crumbs
	Blue sugar crystals
⅓	stick Fruit Stripe gum
1	gumball
	Paper umbrella

Frost half of the cupcake blue (making waves if you like) and the other half white. Spread the graham cracker crumbs over the white side of the cupcake to resemble sand. Spread blue sugar crystals on the blue side. Top with a Fruit Stripe beach chair, a beach (gum) ball, and a paper umbrella.

Rocket Cake

SURPRISE YOUR CHILD with a rocket cake that'll make his spirits soar on his special day. Our out-of-this-world dessert will be the centerpiece of your space party.

WHAT YOU NEED

1 baked 13- by 9- by 2-inch cake
2 to 3 cups white frosting
   Red and blue M&M's
   Red gel icing
   Candles

WHAT YOU DO

To construct this high-flying cake, cut and assemble the baked cake as shown. Cover the cake with the white frosting. Set in place red and blue M&M's for rivets and pipe on red gel icing letters.

For added flair, insert candles in the bottom of the rocket, light, and let them burn briefly (with adult supervision, of course) before cutting and serving the cake. Serves 8 to 10.

Tip: You can cut the longer, unused cake pieces into smaller chunks and place them around the rocket for space junk.

Fire Engine Cake

Your junior firefighter will get all fired up when he sees this hook-and-ladder cake, complete with gumdrop lights, cookie wheels, and a pretzel-stick ladder. Like all fire trucks, it'll "go" fast.

WHAT YOU NEED

- 1 baked 13- by 9- by 2-inch cake
- 6 cups red frosting
- ¾ cup chocolate frosting
- Red M&M's
- Chocolate sandwich cookies
- Pretzel rods and sticks
- Yellow gumdrops
- Black Jelly bean
- White Chiclets
- 1 Black Jujube
- Mini Jawbreakers
- Black twist and shoestring licorice

WHAT YOU DO

Cut the baked cake into four pieces (A, B, C, and D) as shown. Slice B in half horizontally to create E. Frost A and C onto D for the engine bed, as shown, B onto C for the cab, and E onto D for the control panel. Frost the bed and cab red and the control panel brown.

With a dab of frosting, attach an M&M to the center of each cookie to make the wheels, then press onto the engine. Add a pretzel ladder, gumdrop emergency lights, jelly bean horn, Chiclet headlights, and Jujube and jawbreaker controls. Use twist licorice to make a hose and shoestring licorice to outline the windows of the cab. Serves 10 to 12.

Cupcake Tea Set

WHETHER YOU INVITE the March Hare or your best friend to the tea party, this cupcake tea set is the perfect thing to serve. Similar sets were sent in by two *FamilyFun* readers. Carrie Sharp of Suttons Bay, Michigan, celebrated her daughter Audrey's sixth birthday with the "teacups" plus PB & J tea sandwiches. It was also teatime in San Antonio, Texas, where Andrea Schaper made teapot cupcakes, and her husband played the proper British butler, accent and all, for their daughter Alexandrea's sixth birthday.

WHAT YOU NEED

Teacup

1 baked cupcake, unwrapped
White frosting
Red shoestring licorice
M&M's Minis
1 sour ring
Brown gel icing

Teapot

2 baked cupcakes, unwrapped
White frosting
1 sour ring
1 gumdrop
Red shoestring licorice
M&M's Minis
1 candy cane, broken in two

WHAT YOU DO

To make a teacup, frost the sides of the cupcake white. Use the shoestring licorice to create the base and rim. Add some M&M's Minis (or any other candies you like) around the side. Cut off about one third of the sour ring and insert the rest into the side of the cupcake for a handle. Make the tea with gel icing (brown gel for black tea or mix brown and white gel icing for tea with milk).

For the teapot, glue two cupcakes together top to top with a dab of frosting. Cover the sides and top with more frosting. Place the sour ring and gumdrop on top for a lid. Embellish with licorice and candy, as you did for the teacups. Then, insert the straight end of the candy cane at an angle for the spout and the curved end sideways for a handle. Serves 4. (For each additional guest, make another teacup.)

Apron Cake

AT A COOKING PARTY, this dessert really takes the cake. You can make it a day before the party with the guest of honor or turn the frosting and decorating into a party activity with the entire group.

WHAT YOU NEED

1 baked 13- by 9- by 2-inch cake
2 to 2½ cups white frosting
   Red shoestring licorice
   Plastic toy kitchen utensils (or other plasticware, trimmed to size)
   Decorators' icing

WHAT YOU DO

Set the baked cake on a serving platter. Cut away the upper corners of the cake to form an apron shape. Frost the cake with the white frosting. Stick shoestring licorice into the top of the cake to form the neck strap and into the sides of the cake to form the apron strings. Then outline the entire apron with licorice.

Stick a tiny plastic fork and spoon into the apron in the lower left side of the cake. Using the decorators' icing and a writing tip, outline the shape of the pocket as a guide, with the utensils poking out the top. Form the pocket with a mound of decorators' icing and smooth out well. Use the icing to write "What's Cooking?" on the apron. Serves 10 to 12.

Party Plan

"For our cooking party, we sent out invitations on recipe cards. When the kids arrived, we gave them homemade chef's hats and they cooked up their own mini lasagnas. The best part was the apron cake."

— Sharon Cindrich
FamilyFun writer

Pirate Ship Cake

THE STAFF AT *FamilyFun* magazine gave this Pirate Ship Cake, created by Centreville, Virginia, mom Karen Terry and her son, Gregory, a resounding pirate-style "Yar!" We loved Karen and Gregory's ingenuity and the simple design of this swashbuckling confection.

WHAT YOU NEED

2 baked 9- or 10-inch round cakes
3 to 4 cups chocolate frosting
   Chocolate wafer sticks (such as
      Pepperidge Farm Pirouette cookies)
   Milk chocolate wafer rolls (Waffeletten)
   Several sheets of yellow paper
3 10-inch wooden skewers
   Malted milk balls
   Rolo candies
   Root beer barrels
   Plastic pirate figures

WHAT YOU DO

Cut each cake in half, then frost the tops of three of the halves. Stack the pieces, as shown, so the top and bottom of the stack are frosting-free. Trim the curve of the stack so it sits flat when turned on its side, as shown. Cover the cake with the chocolate frosting, then create planking lines along the hull with a butter knife. Chill for 1 hour.

Use dabs of frosting to anchor wafer stick gunwales along the edges of the deck. Press the wafer rolls into both sides of the ship for cannons. Cut sails from the paper, then slip them onto the skewers and set the masts in place. Add malted milk ball cannonballs, Rolo gold booty, root beer barrels, and a few pirates to keep watch.

For safety, place the candles in the cannons, far from the paper sails. Also make sure that the surface on which the cake rests is impervious to wax, as the burning candles will drip. Serves 10 to 12.

Mermaid Cake

THE KIMMEL FAMILY of Montebello, New York, sent us the blueprint for this outstanding mermaid cake, which is large enough to feed a big group of seven-year-olds at a mermaid party.

WHAT YOU NEED

- 1 baked 8-inch round cake
- 1 baked 13- by 9- by 2-inch cake
- 12 baked cupcakes
- 4 cups green frosting
  Necco wafers (pink, green, and purple)
- 2 cups white frosting
- 2 blue M&M's
  Black shoestring licorice
  Fruit leather
- 2 cups yellow frosting
  Colored sugar

WHAT YOU DO

Cut the cake as shown below and arrange as shown at top. Frost the mermaid's tail green and cover it with Necco wafers. Frost the head and body white and the bikini top green. Add eyes made from green Necco wafers and blue M&M's, licorice eyelashes, and a fruit leather mouth. Frost the cupcakes yellow. Sprinkle colored sugar on the hair, the bikini top, and the tail for a marine sheen. Serves 20 to 24.

25

Panda Cake

FOR YOUR PRESCHOOLER'S next birthday bash, bake a cake that looks like his favorite stuffed animal. He and his pals will stuff themselves silly. **Tip:** For a Teddy Bear Cake, lose the white spots and frost the entire cake light brown.

WHAT YOU NEED

- 1 baked 8-inch round cake
- 1 baked 9- or 10-inch round cake
- 4 baked cupcakes
- 1½ cups white frosting
- 2 cups dark chocolate frosting
- 1 mint patty
- Hershey's Mini Kisses
- 1 Junior Mint
- Fruit leather
- Black shoestring licorice
- 2 sour rings
- 2 brown M&M's
- White sprinkles or shredded coconut

WHAT YOU DO

Use the 8-inch cake for the panda's head. Trim the edge of the larger cake to create a scooped neckline and fit it snugly against the head, as shown. Cut 2 cupcakes in half; use 2 halves for ears and 2 for front paws. Use the remaining 2 cupcakes for rear paws. Spread on the frosting, creating light and dark patches of fur, as shown on page 26. Cut the mint patty in half and place one half in the middle of each ear. Add Mini Kisses for claws, a Junior Mint nose, a fruit leather tongue, a shoestring licorice mouth, and eyes made of the sour rings and M&M's. Top the paws with white sprinkles or shredded coconut for added fur. Serves 12 to 14.

Cub Cake

Beware these paw-print cupcakes walk away fast!

WHAT YOU NEED

- 1 baked cupcake
- White frosting
- 1 small mint patty
- 3 Junior Mints or chocolate chips

Spread each cupcake with white frosting. Top the cupcake with the mint patty. Then place three Junior Mints or chocolate chips around the patty to make a paw.

Choo-choo Train Cake

FamilyFun READER Shelley Collette of Palisade, Colorado, engineered this great railcar cake, which makes an ideal centerpiece for a toddler's choo-choo train party. If you invited the entire nursery school, bake extra cars.

WHAT YOU NEED

- 5 baked mini loaf cakes
- 4 cups frosting (any four colors)
- 16 M&M's
- 16 chocolate sandwich cookies
  Cookies and candies
  Red shoestring and twist licorice
- 1 marshmallow, frosted and rolled in sprinkles
- 6 popcorn pieces or mini marshmallows threaded on a wire
- 1 vanilla wafer cookie

WHAT YOU DO

Cut one loaf cake as shown at top left. Use frosting to attach the pieces to the tops of the remaining four loaves (see below left). Frost the engine and cars different colors. With a dab of frosting, place an M&M in the center of each cookie to make the train wheels, then press the wheels against the sides of the train. Make windows on the cab with shoestring licorice. Add cookie and candy cargo, outlined with twist licorice, a marshmallow smokestack with popcorn steam, and a decorated vanilla-wafer engineer. Serves 8 to 10.

Baseball Cap Cake

IF YOUR CHILD eats, sleeps, and breathes baseball, this cake is for him or her. Invite a group of baseball fans to play a few innings, serve up ballpark dogs and popcorn, then cap off the party with this cake.

WHAT YOU NEED

- 1 baked 8-inch round cake
- 1 dome cake (baked in a 1½-quart bowl)
- 3 cups frosting (blue and red)
  Red shoestring licorice
- 1 red gumdrop
  Red M&M's

WHAT YOU DO

Cut a piece shaped like a brim from the 8-inch cake and arrange it next to the dome cake, as shown. Discard the extra piece. Frost the hat blue and the brim red (or the colors of your child's favorite team). Add shoestring licorice to the crown with a gumdrop button. Form your child's initial in M&M's. Serves 6 to 8.

Baseball Cupcake

This cupcake will score a home run with the kids on your child's birthday team.

WHAT YOU NEED

- 1 cupcake
  White frosting
  Red shoestring licorice
  Chocolate frosting

Frost the cupcake white. Using the stitching of a real baseball as your guide, re-create the pattern with the licorice (or with red frosting and a writing tip). With chocolate frosting and a writing tip, sign the ball with the name of your child's favorite player.

Ice-cream Pool Cake

EVERY PARENT wants his or her child's birthday to go swimmingly.
So when *FamilyFun* reader Gail Fournier's son, Scott, turned seven, Gail
was hot for a poolside bash. The coolest part of the party was the cake,
modeled after the aboveground pool in their New Hampshire backyard.
Your kids, like Scott's party guests, will dive right into this ice-cream cake.

WHAT YOU NEED

- ½ gallon premium-quality ice cream
- 32 fudge stick cookies (plain or chocolate-peanut butter)
- 2 cups heavy cream
- ¼ cup confectioners' sugar
- ½ teaspoon vanilla extract
-   Blue food coloring
-   Gummy rings
-   Gobstoppers
-   Paper umbrella
-   Plastic swimmers
-   Red twist licorice
-   Decorators' icing

WHAT YOU DO

Begin by making the ice-cream base.
Let the ice cream soften at room
temperature for 15 to 20 minutes,
then spoon it into an 8-inch round
springform pan, soufflé dish, or plastic container. Pack the ice cream into
the mold and smooth out the top.
Cover with plastic wrap and freeze
for at least 4 hours or overnight.

After the ice cream has frozen solid,
unmold it by dipping the container
quickly into a pan of hot water;
if necessary, you can also loosen the

edges of the ice cream with a knife.
Invert the mold onto a large plate and
carefully lift off the pan to reveal the
ice-cream cake, as shown.

Carefully place the fudge sticks
(we alternated plain and chocolate–
peanut butter) around the sides of the
cake so they resemble the panels of
an aboveground pool. Return the cake
to the freezer.

To make the blue whipped-cream
waves, beat the heavy cream with
an electric mixer until it thickens and
soft peaks form. Add the confectioners' sugar and vanilla extract to the
cream and beat until stiff. Mix in
several drops of blue food coloring.
Frost the top of the frozen cake with
the blue whipped cream, then return
it to the freezer for 15 to 30 minutes
or until set.

Create a lively pool scene with
gummy ring inner tubes, Gobstopper
beach balls, a paper umbrella, and
plastic swimmers. Add a licorice
ladder with licorice rungs (use decorators' icing to glue it together).
Serves 10 to 12.

Worm Cupcake

This cupcake will be a hit with just about any kid who loves dirt, bugs, or nature.

WHAT YOU NEED
- 1 cupcake
  Chocolate frosting
  Chocolate cookie crumbs
- 2 gummy worms

Frost the cupcake and sprinkle on the cookie crumbs for dirt. Use a small knife to make holes in the cupcakes, then stick in the worms.

NATURE

Bug Mountain Cake

AS WE DUG through the cake designs we've received from *FamilyFun* readers, we found two equally earthy creations — a Bug Mountain cake for Nathan Strong of Newark, Ohio, and the centerpiece for Jake Parrott's "creepy, crawly, slimy, icky" fifth birthday party in Charlotte, North Carolina. We couldn't choose between the two, so we combined aspects of each to create this delicious dirt pile. **Tip:** For the dirt, you can pulse the cookies in a food processor, as Nathan's family did, or triple-bag the cookies and dance on them, as Jake's family did.

WHAT YOU NEED
- 1 dome cake (baked in a 2-quart bowl)
- 1 baked 13- by 9- by 2-inch cake
- 3 to 4 cups chocolate frosting
- 2 to 3 cups crushed chocolate cookies (we combined chocolate graham crackers, fudge cookies, and chocolate wafer cookies)
  Plastic bugs, spiders, snakes, and butterflies, washed and dried

WHAT YOU DO
Arrange the dome cake on the rectangular cake, as shown below, securing with frosting. Cover the cakes with the frosting, then sprinkle on the cookie crumbs. Decorate with the plastic bugs, spiders, snakes, and butterflies. (For safety, remove the toys before serving.) Serves 12 to 14.

Pink Pony Cake

THIS FANCIFUL PONY is sprinkled with a little magic — a dusting of edible glitter. Although our pony looks pretty in pink, yours could be frosted with any of your child's favorite colors.

WHAT YOU NEED

2   baked dome cakes (baked in a 1½-quart bowl)

2   cups pink frosting

Edible pink glitter or coloring dusts, available at party stores

Pink sour tape

3   Milk Duds

White Good & Plenty

Black and red shoestring licorice

Silk flowers

WHAT YOU DO

Place one dome cake rounded side up on a tray. Cut and arrange the second cake as shown to create the pony's nose and ears. Ice the entire cake with pink frosting, then dust it with edible pink glitter. Curl strips of pink sour tape by wrapping them around a wooden spoon handle. Arrange them in place to create a flowing mane. Complete the pony using Milk Duds for the eye and nostrils, white Good & Plenty for the ear lining, black shoestring licorice for the eyelashes, red shoestring licorice for the mouth, and a sour tape eyelid. Adorn the mane with silk flowers. (And don't forget to remove them before serving!) Serves 8 to 10.

Party Plan

At a magical pony party, the birthday girl and her friends will love playing Pin the Tail on the Pony, crafting magic pony wands, then kicking up their heels and prancing like ponies. Send guests home with ponytail holders, pony stickers, and mini toy ponies.

Erupting Volcano Cake

FamilyFun reader Caroline Huntress of Cos Cob, Connecticut, concocted this volcano cake for her son Alessandro Chillé's paleontology-themed fifth birthday party. She turned her mom's lollipop recipe into gushing red lava for the ultimate effect.

WHAT YOU NEED

- 1 dome cake (baked in a 4-quart bowl)
- 1 dome cake (baked in a 2-quart bowl)
- 1 baked cupcake
- 3 to 4 cups chocolate frosting
- 1 to 2 cups nondairy whipped topping
  Lollipop Lava (recipe below)

Lollipop Lava

- 1 cup sugar
- 1/2 cup light Karo syrup
- 1/4 cup water
  Red food coloring

WHAT YOU DO

Arrange the cakes and cupcake as shown above, using frosting to secure them in place. Trim the top dome cake as shown at right, then cover the cakes with the frosting. Just before serving, drop a cloud of whipped topping around the crown of the cake and add the Lollipop Lava. Serves 15 to 18.

Lollipop Lava: In a heavy saucepan, bring the sugar, syrup, and water to a boil (parents only). Continue boiling until the mixture reaches 295° on a candy thermometer. Remove the mixture from the heat and stir in the food coloring until the desired shade is reached. (**Tip:** If you don't have a candy thermometer, melt crushed lollipops or hard candy in a saucepan over medium-low heat.)

Let the liquid cool 1 to 2 minutes before pouring it in randomly shaped spews and puddles onto a foil-covered cookie sheet. Let the lava cool completely before removing it from the foil and positioning it on the cake.

Jurassic Cupcakes

MELISSA SPECHT from Anderson, Indiana, and Jennifer Stansbury from Laramie, Wyoming, both suggested placing small plastic party favors on top of cupcakes. Melissa served cupcakes decorated with plastic turtles, fish, and birds at her daughter's Tropical Island birthday party, and Jennifer perched butterfly hair clips on flower cupcakes. Our version, with a brontosaurus, a mighty Tyrannosaurus rex, and others stomping across the cupcakes, works well for a dinosaur party.

WHAT YOU NEED

1 baked cupcake
White frosting
Shredded coconut
Green food coloring
Small plastic dinosaur (washed)

WHAT YOU DO

Frost the cupcake. To make the "grass," place a handful of shredded coconut in a ziplock bag, add a few drops of food coloring, seal the bag, and shake it. Cover the frosting with grass and top with a dinosaur.

Tip: For a sandy look, use crushed graham crackers or molasses cookies instead of tinted coconut. Small rocks can be made out of chopped nuts.

Checkerboard Cake

You DON'T NEED strategy or luck to pull together this simple checker-board cake. When the gumdrop game pieces are in place, play a game — the winner gets the first slice.

WHAT YOU NEED

2	baked 8-inch square cakes
6	cups white frosting
	Red Fruit by the Foot
12	large yellow gumdrops
12	large green gumdrops
	Black shoestring licorice

WHAT YOU DO

Layer and frost the cakes. Using a knife and a ruler, lightly mark a grid of eight by eight squares. Cut the Fruit by the Foot into 32 squares and place them on the cake, as shown. Set up the gumdrop playing pieces and outline the board with licorice. Serves 8 to 10.

Tic-tac-toe Cupcakes

FAMILYFUN READER Kim Arant from Lawrenceville, Georgia, sent us this idea for a quick game of cupcakes. It's the perfect decorating project for a younger child and an excellent centerpiece for a game-themed party.

WHAT YOU NEED

10 baked cupcakes
   Any color frosting
 5 sour rings (or LifeSavers)
10 1½-inch pieces of Twizzler
   Pull-n-Peel candy
 4 orange Starburst Fruit Twists
 4 yellow Starburst Fruit Twists

WHAT YOU DO

Frost the cupcakes. Place a sour ring *O* on five of the cupcakes. Make an *X* with the Twizzler Pull-n-Peel candy on the remaining five, as shown. Place the yellow and orange Starburst Fruit Twists in a tic-tac-toe grid and arrange the cupcakes. Serves 10.

Outback Jeep Cake

HERE'S AN all-terrain-vehicle cake that will really get your party rolling. The rugged look comes from "mud"-covered tires, licorice roll bars, and two adventurous-looking cookie outbackers.

WHAT YOU NEED

- 2 baked 8½- by 4½-inch loaf cakes
- 2 cups green frosting
- ½ cup white frosting
- 5 chocolate-covered doughnuts
  LifeSavers Gummies
  Black and red shoestring licorice
  Black licorice twists
  Pirouette cookies
  Starburst hard candies
  Sour tape
- 2 white Good & Plentys
  Gummy sours
  Vanilla wafer cookies

WHAT YOU DO

Place one of the loaf cakes right side up. For the Jeep's cab, turn the second cake upside down and cut it in half at a slight angle. Ice the top of one half with green frosting, turn it over, and place it on top of the first cake, as shown. Frost the body and roof of the Jeep green and the windows white.

Place doughnut tires on both sides of the Jeep and a spare on the back; press LifeSavers into the centers of the tires for hubcaps. Outline the doors and make window wipers with shoestring licorice. Use licorice twists for the roll bars, pirouette cookies for the bumpers, Starburst hard candies for the headlights, sour tape for the grille, and white Good & Plentys for the door handles.

For the rugged outbackers, use dabs of frosting to decorate wafer cookies with sour-tape hats, gummy-sour facial features, and shoestring licorice mustaches. For the finishing touch, put a toy crocodile or snake in the trunk. Serves 10 to 12.

Sleepover Cake

SINCE SLEEPOVER parties aren't really about sleeping, let your wide-awake party-goers decorate the cookie faces to match their own features, then tuck them into this sweet bed.

WHAT YOU NEED

- 1 baked 13- by 9- by 2-inch cake
- 4 cups pale pink frosting
- 5 Twinkies
- 2 cups pink frosting
- 5 marshmallows
- 5 vanilla or chocolate wafer cookies
  Gel icing (pink and green)
  Mini jawbreakers
  Pink and green Fruit by the Foot

WHAT YOU DO

Turn the cake upside down and spread a thin layer of pale pink frosting on it. To make the bodies, slice the Twinkies in half lengthwise and place the tops cut-side down on the cake bed as shown. Frost a pink sheet on the top third of the cake, flatten the marshmallows for pillows, and position the wafer faces on the pillows (curly hair and big smiles can be made with gel icing; mini jawbreakers are perfect for eyes). Frost a pale pink blanket over the Twinkies and the remaining cake. To make flowers, use pink and green gel icing. Cut Fruit by the Foot and ruffle it to make a snappy bed skirt. Serves 10 to 12.

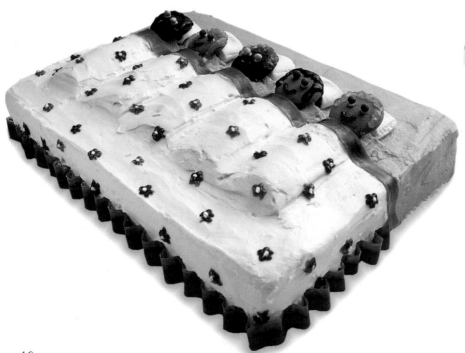

PJ Kids Cupcakes

KIRSTEN SON of South Weymouth, Massachusetts, made these "kid cakes" for her son Patrick's birthday. Patrick unwrapped and sorted the Fruit Stripe gum by color while his dad, Leo, drew the faces with chocolate. The striped shirts reminded us of pajamas, a fitting, though not sleep-inducing, addition to any sleepover party.

WHAT YOU NEED

1 baked cupcake
  White frosting
  Toothpick
1 chocolate chip, microwaved for a
    few seconds to melt
1 Mentos fruit candy
  Fruit Stripe gum (or fruit leather)
  Decorators' icing

WHAT YOU DO

Spread white frosting on the cupcake. Dip the toothpick in the melted chocolate chip and use it to draw a face on the Mentos. To make the shirt, cut a stick of gum in half. Use one half for the body and cut the sleeves from the other half. Attach the Mentos face and add hair with decorators' icing.

Treasure Chest Cake

WHAT PIRATE could resist this chocolate chest overflowing with candy jewels? Instead of bringing the cake out to the birthday table, hide it in your kitchen, then draw a treasure map that leads the band of pirates to the edible loot.

WHAT YOU NEED

- 1 baked 13- by 9- by 2-inch cake
- 6 cups chocolate frosting
  - Chocolate coins
  - Red Fruit by the Foot
  - Mini jawbreakers
  - Candy necklaces
  - Rock candy
  - Rolo candies
  - Hershey's Kisses With Almonds
  - Necco wafers

WHAT YOU DO

Cut two triangular wedges out of the center of the cake; the two remaining pieces will form the bottom and top of the chest. Place the wedges on the bottom half of the chest, as shown, to keep it wedged open, and frost. To add further support for the top of the chest, stand a few large gold coins under the lid. With the hinged end (the piece slanting down) at the back, place the top of the chest on the bottom and frost the entire cake. Wrap the fruit leather straps around the chest and press mini jawbreaker nails into the frosting along the sides of the straps. Fill the chest and the surrounding area with the candy loot and jewels — the more riches, the better. Serves 10 to 12.

Goldfish Cupcake

We combined two *FamilyFun* reader ideas for this fishy cupcake. One was from Julie Reimer, whose husband and three sons love to fish in their town of Shoreview, Minnesota. To celebrate their catches, Julie came up with a fruit leather fish design the guys could sink their teeth into. The other idea was from Karin Overby of Greenville, South Carolina, whose idea for a pool party dessert was fish jumping out of the deep blue sea. We think the mixture of Julie's and Karin's ideas is a splashing success.

WHAT YOU NEED

- 1 baked cupcake
  - Blue and white frosting
  - Yellow and red fruit leather (or gummy fish)
  - Button candies (or M&M's Minis)
- 1 sugar eye (see page 11)

Spread the cupcake with blue and white frosting. Cut the fruit leather into a fish shape (or use the gummy fish) and place on the cupcake. Add button candies or M&M's Minis for bubbles, a fruit leather mouth, and a sugar eye (use a dab of frosting to attach the eye).

45

Pizza Cake

For her son's birthday, *FamilyFun* reader M. Lynne Taylor of Tannersville, New York, threw a party at a local pizza parlor. She baked her cake in a disposable pizza pan, and the restaurant gave her a box for displaying it, plus a real pizza wheel for cutting the cake.

WHAT YOU NEED

1 baked 12- or 14-inch round cake (made in a cake or pizza pan)

2 cups red frosting
  Grated white chocolate (or grated coconut)

$^1/_2$ to $^3/_4$ cup fresh or dried fruit, such as fresh blueberries or grapes; slices of banana, strawberry, kiwi, or orange; or dried apple, banana, pear, mango, peach, or apricot pieces
  Pizza box

WHAT YOU DO

To create the look of pizza sauce, cover the cake, within ½ inch of the edge, with the red frosting. Sprinkle on white chocolate or coconut cheese, strawberry pepperoni, banana mushrooms, grape olives, and so on. Present the cake in a pizza box. Serves 5 to 6.

Burgers and Dogs Cupcakes

FAMILYFUN READER Nancy Wallace of Maryville, Tennessee, has been decorating cakes since she was in fourth grade. Now her four children are getting a taste of their mom's talent on a smaller "canvas." Just check out these "hot dogs" and "hamburgers" with candy condiments — perfect for a cookout party.

WHAT YOU NEED

Baked cupcakes
White frosting
Multicolored nonpareils

Hamburger

Vanilla wafer cookies
Keebler Grasshopper cookies
Yellow and red decorators' icing
Green tinted coconut
Slices of green gumdrop (optional)
Orange juice or lemonade concentrate
Sesame seeds

Hot Dog

Circus peanuts
Caramel squares
Yellow decorators' icing
Cut-up green gumdrop (optional)

WHAT YOU DO

Frost the cupcakes white and set aside. Next, build the hamburgers and hot dogs. For each burger, start with an upside-down vanilla wafer. With a dab of frosting, attach the Grasshopper cookie. Add a squirt of yellow decorators' icing for mustard, a squirt of red icing for ketchup, a sprinkle of tinted coconut for lettuce (to make, place shredded coconut in a ziplock bag, add a few drops of green food coloring, seal the bag, and shake it), and 2 thin slices of a green gumdrop for pickles (optional). Top with the second vanilla wafer, right side up (glue on with frosting if needed). Rub the top bun with juice concentrate, then sprinkle with sesame seeds. Set the burger on top of a frosted cupcake and sprinkle on the nonpareils.

For each hot dog, make the bun by cutting a wedge out of a circus peanut. If the caramel is soft, roll it into a hot-dog shape. If it's hard, first soften it in your hand or in a microwave for a few seconds. (Caution: The caramel can get hot!) Place the hot dog in the bun and squirt on a squiggly line of yellow decorators' icing for mustard. Garnish with green gumdrop relish, if you wish. Place the hot dog on top of a frosted cupcake and sprinkle on the nonpareils.

Dump Truck Cake

A TOY TRUCK, loaded with cake and cookie crumb "dirt," is the perfect treat to unload at a preschooler's construction party.

WHAT YOU NEED

2 baked 8- or 9-inch round cakes
2 3-ounce packages prepared chocolate pudding
3 to 4 cups chocolate cookie crumbs
Clean plastic toy dump truck and shovel

WHAT YOU DO

Cut the cakes into 3-inch-long slices as shown, then cut them in half. Layer the cake, pudding, and crumbs in the clean dump truck and serve with the shovel. Serves 10 to 12.

Tip: For a dessert and take-home favor all in one, fill individual small toy dump trucks (about 6 inches long) with a cupcake and 2 to 3 tablespoons of cookie crumb dirt. Be sure to wash out the dirty trucks before sending them home.

Racetrack Cake

RANDY HARRIS of Weyers Cave, Virginia, created this speedy raceway cake for son Tyler's eighth birthday. Decorating birthday cakes — wife Rhonda bakes them — for his three boys is a family tradition for Randy, whose dad, Paul, did the same. *FamilyFun* judges liked the simple design and the pit-stop-fast assembly.

WHAT YOU NEED

- 2 baked 9-inch round cakes
- 3 cups white frosting
- 1 to 2 cups finely crushed chocolate cookie crumbs
- 1 to 2 cups green sprinkles
  White Good & Plenty
  Checkered paper or ribbon
- 2 toothpicks and tape
  New toy cars, washed with soap and water

WHAT YOU DO

Cut a small semicircular notch from one cake, then position the cakes as shown and cover them with the white frosting. Place a small bowl in the center of each cake and sprinkle cookie crumbs around them to create the track. Remove the bowls and put ¼ cup of sprinkles onto each frosting circle, then press the remaining sprinkles onto the sides of the cake for grass. Lay a white Good & Plenty dotted line along the track and use a pastry bag to pipe a white frosting border around the edge of the cake. Create racing flags by taping small squares of the paper or ribbon to the toothpicks and place them and the racecars on the track. Serves 10 to 12.

Ballerina Cake

PARTY GUESTS will twirl at the sight of this ballerina, dressed in a cotton candy tutu. *Take note:* the cake is big enough to feed an entire dance troupe.

WHAT YOU NEED

- 1 baked 12-inch round cake
- 1 baked 13- by 9- by 2-inch cake
- 16 Twinkies
- 6 cups pink frosting
- 6 cups chocolate frosting
  Chocolate sprinkles
- 2 Junior Mints
- 1 orange gumdrop
- 2 pink Necco wafers
- 1 red jelly fruit slice
  Candy necklace
- 3 small bags pink cotton candy
  Red shoestring licorice

WHAT YOU DO

To form the body and head of the ballerina, cut and arrange the cakes as pictured. Add the Twinkie legs as shown, trimming them if necessary. Frost the leotard and the two Twinkie shoes pink. Spread the head, arms, and legs of the ballerina with chocolate frosting. Fashion the hair from sprinkles. Add the two Junior Mints for eyes, the gumdrop for a nose, the Necco wafers for rouge, and the fruit slice for a smile. String a candy necklace around the ballerina's neck and fluff the cotton candy for her tutu. Finally, lace up her ballet slippers with shoestring licorice. Serves 20 to 24.

Balloon Cupcakes

WHETHER YOU'RE planning a circus party
or a neighborhood penny carnival, this bunch
of colorful balloons makes a festive ending.
Be sure to make a balloon for every child
at the party.

WHAT YOU NEED
>   Baked cupcakes
>   Frosting (equal amounts of yellow,
>   green, blue, and red)
>   Curly ribbon (yellow, green, blue,
>   and red)

WHAT YOU DO
Frost the cupcakes yellow, green,
blue, and red and arrange them
on a large platter or cake cardboard.
Tape a length of ribbon to the bottom of each cupcake. Tie all the
ribbons together and curl the ends
as shown. **Tip:** Cover your cake
cardboard with sky blue wrapping
paper and arrange the balloons
on top so they look like they are
flying up in the air.

Puppy Dog Cake

Your little pups won't be able to keep their paws off this sweet canine cake.

WHAT YOU NEED

- 2 baked 9-inch round cakes
- 2 baked cupcakes
- 4 cups white frosting
  Red Fruit by the Foot
- 1 green Necco wafer
  Junior Mints
  Small mint patties
  Black shoestring licorice
- 2 gray Necco wafers
- 2 blue M&M's

WHAT YOU DO

Layer and frost the round cakes and the two cupcakes. Wrap Fruit by the Foot around the top edge of the cake to make the dog's collar. For the doggie tag, add a green Necco wafer. Place three Junior Mints on the edge of each cupcake paw, one on the top of the cake for the nose, and the rest in a random pattern on the top and sides of the cake. Fill out the spots with a few mint patties, outline the ears and jowls with the shoestring licorice, and add a Fruit by the Foot tongue. Finally, attach the M&M's to the gray Necco wafers with frosting for a pair of sweet puppy dog eyes. Serves 10 to 12.

Bowling Cake

KIDS AT YOUR bowling party will be pinned to their seats when you break out this clever bowling-pin-and-ball birthday cake.

WHAT YOU NEED

- 2 baked 13- by 9- by 2-inch cakes
- 1 dome chocolate cake (baked in a 2½- quart bowl)
- 2 cups white frosting
- 2 cups chocolate frosting
- 3 tea light candles
  Red Fruit by the Foot
  Red decorators' icing

WHAT YOU DO

Arrange one 13- by 9-inch cake on a large platter or cake cardboard. Slice a rectangle off the bottom of the second 13- by 9-inch cake and place it below the first cake as shown in A. Trim the cake into a bowling pin, as shown in B, and spread with white frosting. Add a Fruit by the Foot stripe.

To create the bowling ball, first cut out a circle from the remaining piece of the second 13- by 9-inch cake. To do this, trace around the bowl that your dome cake was baked in with a knife. Place the circle on top of the pin cake, spread chocolate frosting on it, and top with the dome cake as shown in C. Trim around the cake sides to make a smooth ball shape.

For the finger holes, scoop out three circles on the bowling ball and place a tea light candle in each hole. Cover the bowling ball with chocolate frosting. Print your child's name and age with red decorators' icing. Serves 20 to 24.

Camp-out Cake

THIS CAMPSITE CAKE with a gumdrop flame is sure to warm up your party. If possible, let each child decorate one sleeping camper in his or her likeness.

WHAT YOU NEED

Cake
- 2 baked 9-inch round cakes
- 4 cups green frosting
- Graham crackers
- Pretzel sticks
- Gumdrops (yellow and red)
- Decorators' icing
- Gel icing
- Necco wafers
- Chocolate cookie crumbs
- Marshmallow trees (see recipe below)

Marshmallow trees
- 16 large marshmallows
- 2 tablespoons butter
- Green food coloring
- 2 cups cornflakes
- Cooking spray
- Waxed paper

WHAT YOU DO

Layer the cakes and frost them green. Build a campfire with graham cracker crumb ashes, pretzel stick logs, and gumdrop flames. For the campers' sleeping bags, frost graham cracker quarters with bright colors and decorate with gel icing. Draw a camper's face with the two types of icings on a Necco wafer and place on top of each sleeping bag.

Arrange the campers around the fire and add a sprinkle of cookie dirt and a few marshmallow trees. Serves 10 to 12.

Marshmallow trees: In a saucepan over medium heat, melt the marshmallows with the butter, stirring constantly. Remove from the heat and add the green food coloring and the cornflakes, stirring well after each addition. Spray hands with cooking spray and mold cone-shaped trees. Place trees on waxed paper to cool.

Slippery Snake

WHEN THIS scrumptious serpent slides its way onto your table, guests will s-s-s-s-squeal with delight.

WHAT YOU NEED

2   baked ring or bundt cakes
5   cups green frosting
2   blue gumballs
    Red Fruit by the Foot
    Yellow round candies, such as
      M&M's, Necco wafers, or
      nonpareils

WHAT YOU DO

Cut the rings or bundt cakes in half and arrange them in a slithery pattern, frosting the pieces together. Carve a little cake off the sides of one end to make the nose, then frost the entire snake. Add the gumball eyes and a Fruit by the Foot tongue. Decorate the rest of the body with yellow candy spots. Serves 10 to 12.

Pyramid Cake

FOR THE BIRTHDAY child who loves making models, build this pyramid cake that has a surprise buried inside — a cache of sweet treasures.

WHAT YOU NEED

1 box prepared yellow cake mix
1 17¼- by 11½- by 1-inch
    jelly roll pan
  Gold-wrapped candies, such as
    Rolos, Hershey's Kisses With
    Almonds, Hershey's Nuggets,
    and chocolate coins
4 cups white frosting
  Brown sugar

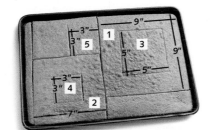

WHAT YOU DO

Butter and lightly flour the jelly roll pan. Pour in the cake mix batter and bake for 20 minutes at 350°. Cut the cooled cake into squares following the diagram at right. Carefully place layer 1 (the 9-inch square) on your serving platter (an extra set of hands may be necessary). Fill the hole in the middle with some of the gold-wrapped candies. Place layer 2 (the 7-inch square) atop layer 1, as shown, spreading a small amount of frosting between them, then fill the hole with the rest of the gold candies. Add layers 3, 4, and 5, securing them with frosting. Use a long knife (parents only) to angle the layers into a pyramid shape. Cover the cake with a layer of white frosting, then use a flour sifter to coat with brown sugar. Serves 10 to 12.

Flutter-by Cupcake

When Robert Davis of Stoughton, Massachusetts, studied butterflies in second grade, his mom, Lonnie, dreamed up this class treat to tie in with the theme. We think these beautifully winged cupcake creatures would also fly off plates at a secret-garden or bug-themed party.

WHAT YOU NEED

1 baked cupcake
  White frosting
½ sour gummy worm
2 jelly fruit slices, sliced in half
  Gumdrop slices (optional)
2 ½-inch pieces of red shoestring licorice

Frost the cupcake and arrange the following on top: a gummy worm body, fruit slice wings (attach the gumdrop detail with frosting, if you like), and shoestring licorice antennae.

58

Butterfly Cake

THIS BUTTERFLY CAKE with candy-coated wings is a sure way to attract friends to a garden birthday party. Let the kids wash it down with nectar (fruit juice).

WHAT YOU NEED

1 baked 8- or 9-inch round cake
2 cups chocolate frosting
1 cup yellow frosting
1 Twinkie
  Jelly fruit slices
  Red Chiclets
  Bull's Eye candy
  Green Skittles
  Red shoestring licorice

WHAT YOU DO

Cut the cake in half, then arrange and frost as shown. Frost the Twinkie and place it between the wings for the butterfly's body. Decorate the wings with candies, and add licorice antennae to the body.

Tip: Hit the candy store with the birthday boy or girl to find candies in his or her favorite colors. Buy candy by the quarter pound so you don't get more than you need. Serves 5 to 6.

Flower Garden Cake

If you're looking for a fun way to celebrate a spring birthday, this colorful crop of flowers really takes the cake — and a few cupcakes, too.

WHAT YOU NEED

- 1 baked 13- by 9-inch cake
- 2½ to 3 cups white frosting
- 4 baked cupcakes
- 5 baked mini cupcakes
- ¼ cup green frosting
- Green gel icing (optional)
- Spearmint candy leaves
- Colored sugars
- Colored nonpareils
- LifeSavers Gummies
- Sour rings
- Jujubes
- M&M's Minis
- Jujyfruits

WHAT YOU DO

First, cover the cake with the white frosting. Arrange the cupcakes and mini cupcakes (you can cut them in half horizontally, for thinner flowers, if you wish) on top of the cake, wherever you'd like a flower. Cover the tops and sides with the white frosting.

Using a pastry bag, pipe a green frosting stem for each flower. If you like, you can also add green gel frosting grass. Place spearmint leaves along the frosting stems, then decorate the cupcakes with colored sugars and candies to create a garden of colorful blooms. You can also pipe on dollops of frosting, as we did on some of our flowers. Serves 16 to 18.

59

Boom Box Cake

WHEN YOU TELL your party guests that it's time for cake, it will be music to their ears — and eyes.

WHAT YOU NEED

- 2 baked 8^1/2- by 4^1/2-inch loaf cakes
- 3 cups yellow frosting
- 2 large mint patties
   Fruit leather
   Assorted candies, such as Pez, Spree, sour rings, Good & Plenty, and Jujubes
- 2 long, thin candles
   Black shoestring licorice

WHAT YOU DO

For the boom box shape, cut off one of the long edges from one loaf cake at a slight angle. Use frosting to stick the 2 pieces to the second cake, as shown. Ice the entire cake with yellow frosting. For the speakers, use a toothpick to score a crisscross pattern on the 2 large mint patties. Cut 2 squares of fruit leather for the tape and CD player lids and use a variety of small candies for the control buttons. Next, add 2 long, thin candles for antennae and outline the cake with shoestring licorice. Serves 10 to 12.

Xylophone Cupcakes

On a scale of one to ten, we think this sweet xylophone will rate a perfect score from music-loving party guests.

WHAT YOU NEED

- 8 mini cupcakes
   Eight colors of frosting
   Red shoestring licorice
- 4 mini M&M's
- 2 mini marshmallows
- 2 thin pretzel sticks

Frost the cupcakes. Line them up on a large platter or cardboard, lay the licorice across the top, and place the M&M's at each end. Fashion the mallets by sticking mini marshmallows onto the ends of the pretzels. Serves 8.

Index

Cake Resources

Wilton Enterprises
www.wilton.com
800-794-5866
Wilton has a plethora of cake-decorating supplies, from the doll used in our Princess Cake to the cake-decorating kit on page 11. They also have a giant selection of theme candles, sprinkles, glitters, and sugars in dozens of different colors. Call or write to order their current *Yearbook of Cake Decorating* ($9.99), or to find a local distributor.

Sugarcraft
www.sugarcraft.com
513-896-7089
This online cake-decorating and candy-supply catalog features more than 20,000 items. They have loads of cake molds as well as the glitter we used for our Pink Pony Cake, and the candy and novelty items we used for the Pool Party, Hawaiian, and Under the Sea cakes. Order items online or visit their retail store at 2715 Dixie Highway (Rt.4), Hamilton, Ohio, 45015.

Photographers

Peter N. Fox: 15 (right)

Andrew Greto: 23

Ed Judice: Front Cover (center), 4 (top), 5, 9, 15 (left), 20, 25, 28, 29 (left), 38, 42, 44, 45 (left), 46, 51, 52, 53, 56, 57, 64, Back Cover (top)

Lightworks Photographic: 27 (right)

Tom McWilliam: 21, 55

Joanne Schmaltz: Front Cover (top left, top right, bottom right), 3, 4 (bottom), 8, 12, 13, 14, 16, 17, 18, 22, 24, 26, 27 (left), 32 (right), 33, 34, 35, 36, 37, 39, 40, 41, 43, 45 (right), 47, 49, 58 (left), 59, 60 (top), 61, Back Cover (bottom)

Shaffer/Smith Photography: Front Cover (bottom left), 6, 10, 11, 19, 29 (right), 30, 31, 32 (left), 48, 50, 58 (right), 60 (bottom), 62, 63

Stylists

Bonnie Anderson/Team, Catherine Callahan, Marie Piraino, Edwina Stevenson, Kimberly Stoney, Laura Torres, Tracy Tucker, Ellen Harter Wall, Lynn Zimmerman

Also from **FamilyFun**

FamilyFun Magazine: a creative guide to all the great things families can do together. For subscription information, call 800-289-4849.

FamilyFun Cookbook: a collection of more than 250 irresistible recipes for you and your kids, from healthy snacks to birthday cakes to dinners everyone in the family can enjoy (Disney Editions, $24.95).

FamilyFun Parties: a complete party planner featuring 100 celebrations for birthdays, holidays, and every day (Disney Editions, $24.95).

FamilyFun Cookies for Christmas: a batch of 50 recipes for creative holiday treats (Disney Editions, $9.95).

FamilyFun Boredom Busters: 365 games, crafts, and activities for every day of the year (Disney Editions, $24.95).

FamilyFun.com: Make the cake that makes the party by visiting us online. Click on Cake Finder to find dozens of creative party cakes.